SEASONS of the RAIN

A Collection of Poems
for the Jewish Woman

JUDY LANDMAN

ISBN: 978-1-0879-1121-2

Cover art:
Miriam Insel
miriam@mayimfineart.com
www.mayimfineart.com

Photo credits:
P. 1: Hannah Domsic on Unsplash
P. 19: Valentin Müller on Unsplash
P. 51: Reginal on Pixabay
P. 67: Juozas Šalna on Wikimedia

Publishing services provided by JewishSelfPublishing. The author acts as the publisher and is solely responsible for the content of this book, which does not necessarily reflect the opinions of JewishSelfPublishing.

www.jewishselfpublishing.com
info@jewishselfpublishing.com
(800) 613-9430

The author can be contacted at seasonsoftherain@gmail.com.

Dedicated in blessed memory of my father, Mr. Jack Margaretten
Yaakov Mordechai Ben Yitzchok Tzvi, a"h
whose precious words were cut short yet still live within me

In appreciation of my mother, Mrs. Klara Margaretten
whose nourishing words replenished those lost

In honor of my husband, children, and granddaughter
who are the words in the story of my life

BAIS YAAKOV SCHOOL FOR GIRLS

RABBI NAFTOLI HEXTER, PRINCIPAL ● RABBI BENJAMIN STEINBERG MIDDLE SCHOOL
443.548.7700 X 210 ● RHEXTER@BAISYAAKOV.NET

Lower Elementary School
Preschool
Rabbi Yitzchok Sanders
Principal

Upper Elementary School
Rabbi Yochanon Stein
Principal

11111 Park Heights Avenue
Owings Mills, MD 21117
443.548.7700
Lower Elementary x 4
Upper Elementary x 3

Rabbi Benjamin Steinberg
Middle School
Rabbi Shaul Engelsberg
Principal

Rabbi Naftoli Hexter
Principal

6300 Smith Avenue
Baltimore, MD 21209
443.548.7700 x 2

Eva Winer High School
Rabbi Yechezkel Zweig
Principal

Rabbi Yehoshua Shapiro
Associate Principal

Mrs. Elise Wolf
General Studies Principal

6302 Smith Avenue
Baltimore, MD 21209
443.548.7700 x 1

Executive Office
Rabbi Zalman Nissel
Chief Executive Office

Rabbi Aaron Gross
Director of Development

Rabbi Yacov Simha
Vice President, Development

6300 Smith Avenue
Baltimore, MD 21209
443.548.7700 x 5

Officers
Dr. Shmuel Markovitz, *President*
Moshe Dov Shurin, *Vice President*
Ofer Lurman, *Treasurer*
Herman Berlin, *Secretary*
Dr. Yoel Jakobovits,
Chair, Va'ad Hachinuch

www.baisyaakov.net
Bais Yaakov is a beneficiary
of the Associated: Jewish Community
Federation of Baltimore

November 12, 2019

To Whom It May Concern,

Mrs. Judy Landman is an articulate artist. The drawings she paints are not with oil, acrylic or colored pencils, but rather with her mighty, saintly pen. The reader of her poetic prose is taken on a journey into the world of the author; a world full of the mundane with a deep eternal lining of spirituality. One cannot but feel uplifted as Mrs. Landman blends the ordinary with the sublime, the mystical with life as it truly is.

Mrs. Landman's writings are intriguing and will find an audience in our community which is hungry for inspiration through Torah true Hashkafa. I highly recommend Mrs. Judy Landman who I have had the privilege to know for many years as a parent of middle schoolers and as a person qualified to provide our readership with a literary experience unparalleled in today's Jewish world.

Sincerely yours,

Rabbi Naftoli Hexter

Rabbi Naftoli Hexter

Rabbi Paysach J. Krohn

117-09 85th Avenue • Kew Gardens, NY 11418   *(718) 846-6900 • Fax (718) 846-6903*
e-mail: krohnmohel@brisquest.com • www.brisquest.com

Chanukah 5780
December 2019

Dear Reader,

Your heart is about to be touched in ways you never thought of before.

The elegant words of poetry by Mrs. Judy Landman will make you pause as one does at the foot of a majestic mountain. The beauty is there to behold but you will wonder, how did this happen?

The words are simple, but are used with creativity and sensitivity. Growing up I always thought a poem had to rhyme, and here they often do, but many times, they do not. That is fine as well because the words and the emotions brought forth are lyrical and touching.

The caress of a baby, the beauty of autumn, the excruciating loss of a beloved parent no longer here, relationships, ambitions, gratitude to our Creator-- they are all presented here on your page, tenderly, like a baby in an open crib lying on a soft blanket, bathed by the warm sunshine coming from the Almighty.

Read some of these poems aloud to your family. They will be moved as you. They will admire her deftness of expression. And for all this we should be grateful to this most capable author.

I wish mazel tov to Mrs. Landman on her great accomplishment and I ask her to please continue writing.

Respectfully,

Rabbi Paysach Krohn

Contents

SUMMER

Preface

Dear Reader,

There is a custom in my family that we write letters of well wishes to the traveler embarking on a journey. This is my letter to you.

The trip you are about to take includes several destinations. Some stops may include visits with family and friends in locations that are familiar, as well as those yet unexplored. It will encompass the new and the old, as you meander along the byways of your own inner world.

Only G-d knows the itinerary of where we are heading. Only He knows how long the trek will take, how smooth or bumpy the path will be. Remember His words to Avraham our patriarch: "*Lech Lecha*—Go for yourself," words that galvanize and encourage.

Seasons of the Rain is a culmination of six years of writing, laughing, and crying throughout the different milestones, seasons, and holidays, life stages of joys and disappointments, challenges and "organic" moments. It has been a voyage into myself that has given voice to the innermost and sometimes silenced expression of self. Some call that the Soul.

Rain is an incredible concept to ponder. The Talmud in tractate *Ta'anis* (7a) states that rain is a source of blessing. We need to pray for rain, and we need to pray for the right kind of rain! Rain is cleansing and life giving, but it can also be overpowering and destructive. Sometimes, the rainstorms that we endure are overwhelming and seem harmful. Other times, they just pitter-patter and lightly fall for seemingly no reason. And yet, it is still a blessing.

G-d gifted us life. Rain is a continuation of all that is good and bestowed with Mercy. However, it is up to us see it as such and to harness it.

There are times that we indeed need protection from the rain. No different than sharing an umbrella during a rainstorm or casting it aside and enjoying a sun shower on your face, *Seasons of the Rain* is a book that will shelter you, dance with you, and perhaps even heal you. We all encounter challenges and personal struggles in our lives. Sometimes, all we want is to feel heard, understood, and accepted. This book will do all that—and much more.

I thank the Master of the World for giving me this wellspring, and I hope it waters your spirit the way it did mine.

THERE ARE MANY WHO need to be acknowledged and thanked, so I will start with above and beyond: Hashem. I thank Hashem for giving me the gift of the pen. As my history teacher, Mrs. E. Lefkowitz, of blessed memory, quoted Sir Edward Bulwer-Lytton: "The pen is mightier than the sword," I pray that I wield it the way He intended.

I thank my dear mother for raising me with love and patience, for listening to me, and making life as sweet as could be despite our circumstances. I thank my father, of blessed memory, for bequeathing my most special heritage of which I am so proud. And really to both of them: *köszönöm szépen* ("thank you" in Hungarian). May this bring you much *nachas*!

Every writer needs her support group. This book was birthed with you, my dear friends, my cheerleaders, and the ones who *really* know me. I thank you all for reading and critiquing and just being there when I sent off yet another e-mail in the wee hours of the night.

To the most incredible organization in the world, staffed by the most incredible people in the world: LINKS! And to think that I found them a mere ten years ago?! LINKS is a peer support organization for children, teens, and young adults who have suffered from the loss of a parent. They do so much more than what you think they do… and even more. My father died shortly before my fifth birthday. It has been a long, sad, and lonely journey on the grief recovery road. LINKS helped shorten that road, made it less lonely, and channeled that pain by encouraging me to write in their magazine. Some poems that you will read first debuted in LINKS magazine.

Every book needs a publisher, and every author needs an editor! Thank you to my publisher, Rabbi Eliyahu Miller of JewishSelfPublishing. And kudos to my editor, Michal Borinstein, and my proofreader, Elisheva Ruffer. I never could have seen this endeavor through without you! The myriad details, for someone who has no clue about the publishing world, were dealt with seamlessly, professionally, and so respectfully to "the diamonds that are my words." For that alone, I am grateful. Thank you, thank you for making my dream a reality.

Some say, "Don't judge a book by its cover," but for this one I say, "DO judge a book by its cover!" Thank you, Miriam Insel, artist par excellence, creative genius, and dear friend, for knowing me oh so well with every colored nuance that I had absolutely no idea how to verbally express and yet you understood. Thank you for your insight and your gift of brush.

I would be remiss if I didn't thank *Binah* magazine for publishing some of my poems and making me somewhat famous!

And finally, thank you to my best friend, my husband, Dovid, for always supporting me and encouraging me, and going the extra mile…"just because."

To my beautiful, wonderful children, each one a true gem. I thank you for sharing the computer with me! Thank you for eating "anything supper"! Thank you for appreciating how so important this project has been to me! I hope I make you proud the way you make me. I love you all.

Judy Landman
Tishrei 5782/Sept. 2021

Between the Raindrops

In between the raindrops
        collect my free-falling tears.

In between the raindrops
        puddle my innermost fears.

In between the raindrops
        drift in gloomy clouds of despair.

In between the raindrops
        I seek shelter called prayer.

In between the raindrops
        open my umbrella of hope.

In between the raindrops
        I finally can cope.

In between the raindrops
        showers cleanse my soul.

In between the raindrops
        mist revives me whole.

For it's within those *raindrops*
I see reflections of the sun.
Shining down upon me, the Holy One.
So open up and cup your hands
Accept these rivulets filled with love
Embrace the rains of blessing
Hugs and kisses from Above.

FALL

collect my free-falling tears…

Seashore's Song

The gentle ocean breeze caresses my arms
as the sounds of my children's laughter tickles my soul.
Warm white sand filters through my toes
like finely sifted flour.

Awash in sunshine
my face radiates the warmth,
that of a long-lasting briquette
winding down in the afterglow of a summer barbecue.

And the roar of the glorious ocean is
but a cacophony yet calm,
each wave standing proudly as it crests
then crashes,

Taking a humble bow
before her audience of gleeful sea fans,
leaving me cold yet warm.

Reviving my senses and awareness
to the Awesomeness
of Hashem's World.

Pinnacles of Glory

Mountains of majesty
Jut upward into the deep blue
Sky that shimmers
From the streaks of Golden* sun.

Peaks reaching infinitely up and beyond
Breathtakingly, each higher than the next,
Crowned by a halo of white…
In a place where Heaven meets Earth.

Evergreens firmly rooted
Coloring the terra landscape forest hues
Standing as proof in testimony to
The Creation.

And proclaiming proudly in praise
To the Master Who willed this all to be
with-one-utterance.

Pondering in awe at the beauty of this world,
Wondrous and so overwhelmingly grateful,
Juxtaposed with
The greatness of G-d
And the smallness of Man,
I humbly admit:
*Bishvili nivra ha'olam.***

My eyes delight!
My being restored to its natural might,
As heart and soul unite and sing:
*Hamechadesh betuvo bechol yom tamid ma'aseih vereishis.****

---

* Golden is a city in Colorado

** "The world was created for me." (*Sanhedrin* 37a)

*** "Who recreates, in His kindness, the creation of the world every single day." (Prayer)

Star Light

The view from Tighlman's Island, Chesapeake Bay on a summer night

A distant speck
composed of gases
and the Ethereal
shines its brilliance upon those who seek
Guidance
in the all-encompassing Darkness
that is Night.

As with the flick of a switch
suddenly, simultaneously
begins the light show in the Heavens
millions of stars surrounding your very being
reducing you to but a speck
as you crane your neck
trying to grasp all that's there
of His Infinite goodness
in this world
and the next
leaving you breathless in awe
at the soundless orchestra in the cosmos
Playing in perfect synchrony
and pure harmony
filling the soul with the sweet taste
of G-d's Milky Way...

*Hashamyim mesaprim kevod Keil,
uma'asei yadav maggid harakia.**

* "The Heavens speak the glory of G-d, and the firmament tells of His handiwork." (*Tehillim* 19:2)

Weather is cooling
winds are blowing
sun's setting a bit earlier,
yet birds chirp
and the kids play outside
but still I get wistful—
summer is over.

School supplies already bought
knapsacks full of potential
new shoes wait patiently in their box
anticipation for what's to come—
summer is over.

Remember then
when
the summer strrrretched before us
possibilities endless
projects finally completed
or started
so much to do!
or not...

Rocking in my egg chair
with book in hand
deliciously drinking in the words
endless sun and slushies
my *"tznius* tan"
summer!

Memories made
memories stored
as I flip through the album
in my mind
recalling all the Great Adventures
with precious ones
reliving the moments

pure joy in my heart—
summer lives on.

Colored leaves
abandoning trees
and rustling of the Soul
Heralds in a new season
with the blast of a ram's horn
essential introspection
of my time in His Time.

Summer's but mere memory
There's work to be done
inside and outside
holding those tear-stained pages
and stirring pots
Praying for a good year!
for me, for you, for all of us.

Bare trees
limbs that freeze
I am a wooly mammoth!
protection from the elements
much like those whispered prayers
keep me warm
with hot cocoa
Here comes Old Man Winter.

A Candle in the Dark
a flame, a spark
ignites inspiration anew
awakening the olfactory
tickling the taste buds
for just one more
(how many did you eat??)
'til the next
stirrings of hope

hidden in the snow
layers below
Life forges on
in the taste of a sweet fig
of the Sacred Seven.

Hold on tight!
It's merry-making season!
Cacophony
of pounding noise
in obliteration!
and cries of delight!
as we play the game
Guess Who in masquerade
and imbibe
baskets filled with love
High yet once again
unity unbottled.

Jack Frost is finally melting
and watering the budding shoots
that crane their petaled necks
skyward perfuming the air
I inhale
incense of blossom and grass
and Mr. Clean
while we scrub and purge
more than the kitchen floor
Gathering all we need
for impending Redemption.

Standing at the Mountain once again,
with my mom's delicious cheesecake
possibilities abound
for glorious growth.

Lush produce
floral fantasy
boundless sun
new memories
projects
Travel
His world
and your inner world—
Oh! Summer.

Mountain Climbing

There's nothing like Elul introspection in the Rocky Mountains.

The summer flew by
in the blink of an eye.
Seasons they change with nary a sigh.
And the cliché is so true,
"Oh! How time flies."
And I wonder...
Did I try?
enough
Did I cry?
enough
To be all that I want to be
to know what I have within me?
The possibility.
Of Humanity.
Reflecting Divinity.

Elul is here.
End of a year.
And I wonder...
Did I do my best?

Did I pass those tests?
To ascertain
That my efforts were not in vain...
I humbly implore You judge the same.

But I know with certainty
How I surely *did* try!
So many tears did I cry!
Pouring forth from the sweat of active
    prayer.
Soul-like muscle stretching with each
    intake of air.
And with every hurdle I perspired.
Inspired,
aspired
to climb higher and Higher
traversing my own path
on this Mountain of Life.
*Mi ya'aleh vehar Hashem, umi yakum
    bimkom kodsho.**

* "Who may ascend the mountain of Hashem, and who may stand in the place of His holiness?"
    (*Tehillim* 24:3)

Turning Point

In commemoration of my father's 40th yahrtzeit

So much inside
how to express
what's in my heart
the great divide
of emotions roiling
tears boiling
from the depths
of my colored blue green eyes
your eyes
Oh, Totty...
or was it Papi?
Forty years
is a very long time
to have my world
my sun
my moon
just die
with the memories
of laughter
together
'round the globe
our home in Spain
and Miami
and even the Borough

family so dear
friends far and near
reflective of my native tongue
an amalgam
English Spanish Magyar
I don't remember any of it
although I've tried
I so badly wish
to open my brain
and remove the trauma
that blocks
to recall
relive
recapture it all
but I can't...
And until then
I cry
wipe and dry
breathe and sigh
bridge the divide
and marvel
at who am I
                    your daughter

Recalibrate

Discombobulate
where is my escape
laboring from eight to eight
can't stay awake
caffeine intake
sugar in my cake
Anxiety awaits
trying to self-placate
as summer dissipates
back to school in haste
this stress creates
butterflies on my plate
I'm so late
soon a *yahrtzeit* date
cry and agitate
deep breaths I take
time to Recalibrate
introspect before it's too late
count my blessings as I wait
for things to abate
after this earthquake
stop the snow-globe shake
For my own health sake
pray and meditate
Appreciate
gently peacefully a new slate
Aaaahhhh
Oh how great
It's Elul
Happy Healthy New Year
I simply state.

Bubblegum

Didja' ever just step in it?
too late to stop
retrace your steps to
avoid it
but now you're stuck in it
a nice big wad
disgusting to think about
where it's been
whose mouth
Ewwww
who invented gum anyway???
find a tissue
start to extricate
pull at it to pull it off

strands of gooeyness
elongate
Like cellular membranes
Ewwww
try again to detach
but it's wedged in real good
and now there's pieces of dirt in it
Ewwww
deep breath and try again
this time with a blunt edge of some sort
plastic knife works just fine
but a knife nevertheless

Scraaaaappppe
it all off
even the little leftover residue
because those are the worst
and most sticky
and muck-attracting
oh!
it's off!
clean Soul!
I mean sole…

Ballad of the Booths

My favorite holiday
when palm fronds sway
caressing perfect citron I pray
judgement sealed and complete
     with honey and apples and all is sweet

Wooden walls that seem flimsy at best
cocoon my family in Hashem's nest
twinkling stars that wink in between
bamboo mats so gentle and serene
swinging golden and olden decorations
     reflecting the love of generations

Warmed by hot chicken soup
Spiced with sparks of
Providence and love recouped
reminiscent of our Desert travel en masse
safely cushioned in first class
     adrift in Clouds of Glory

Forever is our story
we journey now as then
hope for redemption once again
refueling at each festival's station
     anticipating the Final Destination

Hosting Guests and guests galore
eating sweeping crumbs on patio floor
"now you see 'em now you don't"
is not just a cliche nor fun game to play
for Sublime Family join us as we welcome
    and say
     *Azamin liseudasi Ushpizin ila'in.**

Icing on the cake
Velvety covers of Holiness we take
Dancing without stop
Singing joyously is our klopp
From the depths of our soul
The *raison d'etre* that makes us all whole
Candy so pure a real treat
    Matan Torah made us all complete

My *favorite* holiday
My Hebrew true birthday
    Chai Tishrei!

*Ki orech yamim ushnos chaim...***
    *Ein orach chaim ella Torah.****

---

* I invite to my meal the exalted guests. (Prayer said before meals in the *sukkah*)

** "Because [they add] to you length of days and years of life." (*Mishei* 3:2)

*** "There is no life other than Torah." (*Midrash Mishlei* 10)

Angels in My Kitchen

Thank you to Binah for printing this.

Angels in my kitchen keeping me awake
Angels in my kitchen prodding up my back that aches.
Angels in my kitchen stirrin' all my pots
Angels in my kitchen reminding me what's hot.
Angels in my kitchen sprinkling salt and pepper spice
Angels in my kitchen making it smell oh-so-nice.
Angels in my kitchen work that Kitchen Aid
Angels in my kitchen guiding human hands in braid.
Angels in my kitchen flutter in Thursday Night
Angels in my kitchen cooking heavenly delight.
Angels in my kitchen dancing all about
Angels in my Shabbos house,
I gratefully sing and shout—

*"Shalom aleichem, malachei hashareis..."**
And thank you to all my earthly angels in my life!

* "Greetings, ministering angels." (Friday night prayer)

Seventh Heaven

I light the candles usher in their glow
serenity in my home, as peace they bestow
Time seems to stop in that flickering light
as the setting sun melds into twilight.
The clock's ticking stops
slooowwwinng down the frenzied pace.
I sigh in relief, eagerly enveloped in that sublime place.

Is it possible to feel
what is surreal?
G-dliness revealed!
I grasp, I clasp a fervent prayer
for myself, for family and friends,
for my People everywhere.

Wine guggling its recitation
the ancient words of the Creation.
Reminding me,
blessedly,
of the world's purpose,
for Eternity.

Steam rising from its yeastly vessel
fluffy softness warmly nestles.
In between bites
my appetite delights
in this perfect symmetry
the paradox of the earthly and the Holy.

Like the hallway of This World
there's a yearning for what's to come.
Deliciousness; whet-some.
Stirring within me so much more than my sense of taste.
Experiencing joyfully, without haste.

Surrounded at this table by those whom I love
I raise my eyes and thank the One Above.

For granting us this golden treasure-gift
that gives my soul its spiritual uplift.
Recharging my body's battery
replenishing and nurturing it physically.

To grow and do the whole week through.
Acknowledging all comes from You!
And finally, climactically
Epically on Seventh Day,
Proclaim, reclaim in epiphany
I proudly say:
"Vayechulu!"

Footprints

Thank you to Binah for printing this for Parashas Lech Lecha.

To walk where others have walked
With Angels
Always G-d
Surrounded by the vast Land
And stark beauty, a gift for Eternity
That is the Judaean hills
Mountains of Challenge
Witness to battles
and Tests of a Lifetime
fought with Faith
and passed through Prayer
A Promise endowed
In the genetic code
for the Stars and the Sand
now scattered
waiting to be gathered
remnant to what once was
and *still is…*
defying archaeology
Dig deep within
'neath the desert sun
To touch it is to feel
History
Identity
Destiny
Find the paths of greatness
And tread
the Footprints of our Fathers
And Mothers
Forever imprinted
In her holy soil
Forever in my Soul
        Am Yisrael Chai.*

* "The Jewish nation should live."

Dark and Light

Where has the freedom of childhood gone
the innocence of that age
the purity of soul and spirit

who dares to sully my sweet
child
who beholds the breaking
of the bubble
of my baby

bring him back
I yell and scream
and cry
and die
you have killed his G-dliness

with your damning words
crushing of self
painting a scarlet letter
for all to see

for me to bear witness to
for no one to know
who you are
Esther am I
who points to that Haman
of my child's
neshamah.

Pray!
fight and roar
and scream and cry.
I will not die
nor the apple of my eye.
Return him
once more
to the days of yore
with *healing*
time will tell
love will swell
my sweet child
now grown
Resurrected.

WINTER

gloomy clouds of despair…

Candle Prayer

A flicker of darkness
a flicker of sadness
a flicker of pain
and despair.
A Yearning
of learning
of salvation
Mei'ayin yavo ezri?*
A glimmer of light
Miracles might

Radiant flames
of Dedication
one Nation
Redemption
Ezri mei'im Hashem.**

* "From where will my help come?" (*Tehillim* 121:1)

** "My help [comes] from G-d." (Ibid. 121:2)

The Last Candle

strike the match
light the flame
ignite the candle
praise Your Name

gaze into the glow
watch them burn slow
steady and true
so clear the olive hue

reflection in glass
we remember the past
commemorate the *nes*
as Hashem we bless

sing with joy
sing with might
pray with fervor
dance in delight

spin the dreidel
win some gelt
savor the chocolate

before it all melts

eat with gusto
savor the grease
latkes doughnuts
pass more please!

parties are over and families fed
sticky kids straight into bed
but wait...

a lone candle still remains lit
burning brighter and fiercer
refusing to quit
with oil so pure the message is clear:
Never burn out
don't despair
always shine out
for you are that special *Ner*!
Ner Hashem nishmas adam!*
Happy Chanukah!

* "A person's soul is the candle of G-d." (*Mishlei* 20:27)

The Great Sleigh Ride

How precious are the small pleasures, like sledding with your nine-year-old, your youngest child.

I trudge up the hill
In the cold and dark
Holding onto whatever I can
For dear life
It is slippery and steep
As I huff and see the puff
I am at the top
I am afraid
But not so my partner!
He scampers up the hill
With agility and excitement
Anticipating his next flight
I support him in his journey
And hold steady
Off he goes
      Doooowwwwnnnn
Gliding in delight
Coasting over the bumps
He flips once
Lands on his back
Exhilarated!
"Your turn!" he shouts
"I am too old" I want to shout back!
But I don't.
I breathe in his glee
And love
as he helps me
and believes in me
      "AAAIIIIIEEEEEEeeeee "
I wanna another turn!
Life sure is a lot like sledding....

I Am a Tree

Growing
Reaching
Rooting
Stretching
Connecting
Breathing
Beautifying
Shading
Fortifying
Protecting
Strengthening
Supporting
Uplifting
Swaying
Shaking
Falling
Reviving
Striving
Climbing
Maturing
Life Giving
Never Dying
Tu BiShevat

Seed of Splendor

Dedicated to the cultivators of splendid flowers, guided by Hashem's trust in raising His children.

Open up
delicate flower
tightly closed
fisted bud
cloistered color
barbed thorns
rough stem
standing
ramrod straight
unyielding
unforgiving

Open up
delicate flower
unfurl
inner beauty
true colors
bedazzling
soft petals
glistening with dew
sweet scent
gentle fuzz
firmly
budding
growing
upward
pushing
forward
in full bloom

Child in the Corner

Dedicated to Mrs. H.

Child in the corner child in the corner,
why do you sit there so?

Child in the corner child in the corner,
I don't really know.

Child in the corner child in the corner,
breathe and change the flow.

Child in the corner child in the corner,
come and learn and grow.

Child in the corner child in the corner,
be loved and nurtured and it will show.

Child in the corner child in the corner,
salvation will come you too will soon glow.

Child of the world,
Child of Hashem!

*Chanoch lena'ar al pi darko.**

---

* "Train the youth according to his way." (*Mishlei* 22:6)

Sand-catcher

Inspired by my youngest son, Moshe Chaim, on the occasion of his fifth birthday.

Time is flying by
and I feel as if I'm in the proverbial sand glass.
Watching the moments of you, my precious child,
like the others before.
But you are my baby.
And now my five-year-old BIG boy,
growing,
flowing.
As I gaze upon the swiftly moving sand
through the narrow opening.
Like the passage of time, I am in that constriction of Present.
yet—and still—
expanding;
bridging Past to Future.
And I want to crawl and nestle into that narrow space,
snuggle there with you and plug it up.
To catch each grain that is so precious,
to behold *that* granule so dear,
and remember you as then, my sweet baby.
remember you as now, my BIG boy.
For oh too soon!
Like your brothers and sisters before
your deliciousness gliding into Adult.
But forever you will be my baby.
And I will be left with life's hourglass...
filled with *gold*.

Curly Goodness

*Dedicated to my daughter on the occasion of her **bas mitzvah!***

Your curls,
your twirls,
your life-whirls,
sweet growing girl
is my Tova Leah Rochel.
Your zest,
your sparkle,
your blue-eyed twinkle.
Your bright smile and effervescent laughter,
your funny happily ever after
is my Tova Leah.
Your kind nature,
your sensitive stature,
your wisdom beyond-your-years mature
is my Tova Leah.
Your innocence and youth,
your diligence and quest for truth.
Always and forever my good *tuchter*
Hashem's goodness
Tova Leah Rochel.

Vertical Beauty

Beautiful and regal
is my daughter
A curve;
57 degrees
A spinal fusion.
Straight is her strength
Bravery erect
Beautiful and regal
is my *hero*,
my *daughter*,
Chana Miriam

Flight

On the occasion of my daughter's high-school graduation.

She soars
like a newly released bird
spreading her wings in take off
ascending up, up, up
so High
fearlessly
joyously
naturally
inhaling the fresh air
propelling her further
to reach the hovering heavens
kissed by the sun shining on her back
caressed by the fluffy white clouds
coasting in G-d's glorious blue sky
she is free
ready to explore
and navigate her journey
on this earth
choosing her own flight path
in her lifetime
She is ready to fly!

Mazal Tov on graduating high school!

The Storyteller

Dedicated to my son Yaakov on a special birthday.

He has finally arrived.
Nine days late,
nine months of infinity,
but he is here and ours,
and now in *this* world.
His wails are his very first words.
Breath of Life
signaling the end of his cocoon
in the *other* world,
and heralding his foray into Humanity.
A statement forever remembered
that most beautiful sound
and the very first sentence in the story of
his life,
Our life:
the story of a Family.
Many chapters have since been written
storyline unfolding of what's to come
of the expected
and the surprise!
Cliffhangers
Page-turners

Laugh-inducers
and sometimes tears
Tales of the dramatic and pragmatic
sometimes slow and tedious
the natural milestones
of difficulties
Hurdles to overcome
and challenges that frustrate
describing growth
chronicling triumphs
and great Joy
in the saga
of his personal narrative.
yet still ours to record as co-authors.
And now
as his wings finally unfurl
and his beautiful colors are revealed
he can fly
He *will* fly.
It is time for him to write his *own* story.
*Zeh sefer toldos Adam.**

* "This is the account of the descendants of Adam." (*Bereishis* 5:1)

Treasure Trove

Dedicated to my son Joe.

We raise our children to fly
Yet when they spread their wings
We choke up and cry

We want our children to soar
Yet when they do
"Stay back," we implore

We wish that time would freeze
To hold you close
To our family tree

We turn the pages in albums of old
Cherishing, relishing
memories of Gold

And in those moments, truth be told
while raising you and loving too
surprisingly, we ourselves grew

From Whom all good stems
We thank Hashem
For gifting us our precious gems

Each pearl and diamond in our treasure chest
Our children
our lives
We are truly blessed

Hodu laHashem ki tov ki le'olam chasdo!*

---

* "Give thanks to G-d, for He is good." (*Tehillim* 136:1)

Red Balloon

Written on the occasion of the engagement of my son and daughter-in-law! What an incredible milestone! What an incredible feeling!! My joy knows no bounds! And for some reason, the image of a balloon popped into my head!

Like a balloon
filled up with air
propelling higher and Higher
drifting across the sky
so freely
without a care in the world
a splash of color against white and blue
visage of joy
that recalls memories
of childhood enchantment
and the simple pleasures of life
with squeals of delight
"Look! A balloon!"

Shielded eyes
search Heavenward
find it
follow it
as far as one can see
charting its own flight path
until
out of sight
yet not out of mind
for Potential
onward
upward
is what buoys us
to grow

So is my joy
filling me up
Expansively
spreading and sharing
this magic of pure elation
I continue to drift
without a care in this world
splash of color
against the grey clouds of challenge
enchanted by the reminders of
what the simple pleasures *really* are
"Life! A Blessing!"
propelled higher and higher by
oxygen
that is *gratitude*
and what buoys us to grow

*Ivdu es Hashem b'simchah!**

* "Serve G-d with joy." (*Tehillim* 100:2)

Wedding's over
Guests are gone
Sheva brachos done
Dresses returned one by one
and yet I sit here still
like the scattered confetti left in the dark
basking in the warm afterglow
that is forever etched in my mind
sealed in my heart
and forged on my soul
of that most precious moment
when time stood still
much like your hallowed entry into this world
Now the beginning of your sacred new life
as we walked you down that path
treading in those same footprints
from generations so long ago
cocooned in memories of the Eternal
> built on the foundation of our Past
> most precious tradition
> cemented in the Present
> by love, hope, and holiness
> dedicated with a vision for the Future
> an everlasting home.

I am overcome with the *awesomeness* of it all
and so very grateful to witness the perpetuation of the generations
*Shehecheyanu vekiyemanu vehigiyanu lazman hazeh.**

* "[Blessed are You, Hashem, our G-d, King of the universe,] who has kept us alive, sustained us, and brought us to this season." (Jewish blessing)

Mirror Reflections

Dedicated to Rivka Pnina, who made her way into this world on 7 Nissan 5781/March 20, 2021

Looking in the mirror I now see
My mother
And all the other Mothers
Who have paved the path for me
Prayed and hoped
And waited for the very day
They would be
A link in the chain
Of continuity
Looking in the mirror I now see
The Future and the Past
fruits of Eternity
With your very entrance into this world
Present
That you are
your teeny delicious essence
I can't wait to hold to inhale to kiss
As I thank Hashem for
This precious legacy
Looking in the mirror I now see…
      I am a grandmother

Anyának a Kézet

Hungarian for "Mother's Hands"

whose hands have touched
whose hands have bathed
whose hands have held
whose hands have swathed

whose hands have dressed
whose hands have braided
whose hands have buttoned
whose hands have plaited

whose hands have played
whose hands have hooked
whose hands have shopped
whose hands have cooked

whose hands have written
notes of praise
whose hands have signed
absent notes and delays

whose hands have worked
to travel the world
whose hands have embraced
as memories unfurled

whose hands have held hands down the aisle
whose hands have held newborns in celebration
whose hands have prayed in appreciation
whose hands have blessed the next generation

whose hands have cherished
those precious to her
whose hands have given her whole self and more

My Mother's Hands
Anyanak a Kezet
My Mother's Hands
a Divine present

I hold your hand and you hold mine
for this is the way of mothers and children
'til the end of time.

Happy 75th Birthday Mommy/Bobby!

Transcendental

How do you say goodbye when you can't recall saying hello?
How do you try and remember everything that you want to know?

I try to piece together an image of you in my mind
But the inner pain spans years I wish I could revert and unwind
to the times I joyfully waved hello and goodbye,
to a Father who loved me, so real and alive.

That carefree time is tragically ended,
and the path to those memories lays twisted
and bended.

Yet,
the love that You gave me still remains real and alive,
burning within me, warming the will to survive.
A little girl, now a Mother, with impetus to thrive,
to grow and to strive,
and to pass that same love to those whom I dearly love so,
and ever so gratefully kiss
goodbye and hello.

Brotherly Love

Dedicated to none other than my one and only brother.

I don't remember when you were born
But we have pictures
He, swaddled in a blanket
Eyes closed
Sleeping like a baby
In Father's arms
She, in a navy velvet dress
With pearls
Even then... at age three
Hands on hips
Bossy
Big Sister
Oh so proud as can be
Recalling the white and wild
Hair
Climbing everywhere
Allergic to tomatoes
With shouts of
"Yoy! Nem Szabad!"
"Oy! Not allowed!"

Piercing the calm...
Until the calm was pierced
With only Mother cradling
Those bereft
And still...
The wild child
Grew
With his Big Bossy Sister
Intact
Yet broken
allergic to tomatoes
Wild hair no longer
Turned blonde
Heart as BIG as his brawn
Finding his way
Finding our way
With bittersweet memories
My baby brother
 I will always love you.

Hear Me Out

I have heard your voice
but you have not heard mine
We've nary exchanged a spoken word
in this span of time

But to say we've never laughed and bantered
nor had any conversation
Would be a misnomer
on what defines communication!

Paying rapt attention as fingers fly
and lips reply
In the silent language of ASL*
where words *do* matter!
Filled with nuances so rich
far transcending mere audial chatter

With open hearts
to give to those who listen
I have learned so much from you
Mommy and Daddy
How to really pay attention!
to look beyond the superficial
And feel what is truly real
that love can transcend the five senses
Even if you can't *hear.*

* American Sign Language

The Juggler

Emotions overloaded
How do I do this life thing
And juggle all those balls
Each one so precious
Maddening at times
But oh so beloved
My children
My mom
My *morah*-ing
My husband
My home
My own self...
I am the juggler
Par excellence
Or runner up
But dare I drop those balls
And stop the game
For the true juggler knows
To keep an eye on his own
Set of balls
And no one else's
To throw them upwards
to the Heavens
Catching them once again
In his capable hands
securely lovingly joyfully
Held close to His heart
And when it's all over
Take a bow
Smile
I love to Juggle

Pekeleh

Yiddish term for baggage.

Sometimes there is no energy left
to do the right thing
or to do anything at all
leaving you totally confused
bewildered
pent up anger
simmering inside
in all your pores
totally exhausting
draining you and depleting you
from whatever's left in the first place
WHAT exactly are you supposed to do?!?
      Yet ...
sometimes the best thing to do
is NOTHING
Hashleich al Hashem yehovcha veHu yechalkelecha.*

---

* "Cast your burden on Hashem, and he will sustain you." (*Tehillim* 55:23)

Window to My Soul

Dedicated to those who need healing.

Peering out the window of this room
looking out and beyond
or just what's right there in front of me
so close
yet so far away
caged in the jail of my mind
I need to cut
the chains that have surrounded me
and break free
without harming myself
or my soul
help me
be the real me
in this room I cannot call home
someday I will fly and soar
and look through a window
of my very own.

Seamstress

Pain is like a sailor's knot
or not
dare try unfurl and unwind
the different ends and frayed edges
so tangled
pull a little one way
it loosens
pull again
it tightens
constriction so strongly intertwined
a jumble of woven chaos
like yarn
the cheap and ugly kind
who needs this
gentle tugging
feels like forever
is it really worth it
who cares about each strand
no longer smooth and whole anyway
just cut the whole thing off
stab it
with sharp silver shears
the kind kept in a drawer
rip it apart to shreds
until there's nothing left
of your humanity
AAAUUUGH!!!!

is *that* really worth it???

pick up the pieces
delicately
gently
gather the wisps that are left
discarded and forlorn
yet softened by agitation
and yes
even the mutilation of fibers
bind each one together
to reinforce each strand
as it lengthens
strengthens
threading it through
the needle of mend and repair
stitching together
a beautiful tapestry
the Sewing of a Soul.

Surge of Courage

Courage
doesn't look pretty
or neat
or even glamorous

Courage
is not always noticed
and most often exposed
in a private moment
between you and
Someone

Courage
hurts
burns
makes you cry your eyes out
until you have nothing left
so you think …

But You do

Courage
surges
rumbling deep from within
the drip-dropping of a rivulet
inside your soul
streaming forward
gaining momentum as rushing rapids
flowing into a cascading waterfall
harnessing the power and the
strength
that was always there

Find your courage
Find yourself
Find your inner *hero.*

Detangle

*Dedicated to all those **sheitel machers** and hair stylists that help us soooo much.*

Comb
The frizzle
The fuzz
The furl
Brush
Straighten
Smooth out
Every loose curl
Condition
Each strand
No more knots
Just finesse
Shake out the waves
Detangle
The mess
Stroke
so soft
Sleek to the touch

Detangle my life
A little less rough
Aaahhh…
A little limp now
A little flat
Dull—where's the shine?
It's all become matte!
So…
Embrace the knots!
Beribbon each curl!
There is Eternal beauty
In this hairy- Life-whirl!
Personality/Individuality
Opportunity/Creativity
Challenges/Difficulty
Stick with it
Unleash the wave of
Resiliency

Divine Hamantasch

Survival
A miracle tale
simple story
yet not
Redemption's taste
concealed
in that sweet filling
oozing out from within
stickiness leaving its mark
like the very obvious
Omnipresent
Hand of Hashem
Take a bite
Delight
Happy Purim!

Adar Adulation

Dedicated to the great ladies of the Simchas Esther Purim shpiel!

My
Salvation!
Jubilation!
Intense Sensation!
Energetic Excitation!
Enigmatic Exultation!
Magnanimous Elation!
Whoops of Joy Articulation!
Dance and Sing Gesticulation!
Laughter and Tears Combination!
Spread It Here and There Contagion!
*LaYehudim hayesah orah vesimchah vesason viykar—kein tiheyeh lanu!**

Laughter!
Music of the soul
enjoyed alone
but more delicious
when shared with others
can take us to great heights
and feelings of camaraderie
drawing out the hidden from deep within
the Holy sparks of greatness
and catalyst for the Finale
in this endless turbulence we call *galus*:
LaYehudim hayesah orah vesimchah vesason viykar—kein tiheyeh lanu!
Let's laugh together!.

* "'The Jews had light, happiness, joy, and honor' (*Esther* 8:16)—so should we." (*Havdalah*)

The Artisan

From deep within his soul
he strums his violin
plucking each string
in rhythm and harmony
celestial blend of sound
with a purpose

From deep within her soul
she paints each stroke
brushing the canvas
splashes of color
not random
with purpose

From deep within his soul
he raises his voice in song
hitting each note
of lows and highs
in perfect pitch
with purpose

From deep within her soul
she writes her prose
thoughts spilling on paper
choosing each word
in alliteration and rhyme
with purpose

Souls
of searching
of longing
to the Infinite
with deepest reflections

all with Purpose
in serving The Master Artist
and Creator of all Souls

*Kol haneshamah tehallel Kah.**

---

* "Let all souls praise G-d, Hallelukah!" (*Tehillim* 150:6)

In the King's Court

There is *something*
about sitting in shul
hearing the Megillah
listening with your children
looking at the words on yellowed parchment
or shiny glossy paper
for the thousandth time
and still the first
with a new perspective
fresh and exciting
like the crinkling new costume of your six-year-old!
And paying serious attention
to the mitzvah and the *nes*
with the same earnestness of
the coming of age of your *bas-mitzvah* daughter!
While peeling another layer away
with more mature understanding
and search for meaning
Revealing the inner growth
of your own blossoming Rose high school senior
Embraced by a faith and love of your own
from Above
and below
of someone somewhere on the other side of the *mechitzah*
As you sit deliciously squished *together*
on the hard wooden bench that is softened by
years of prayer and tears.
With only the strong solitary voice
of the *ba'al koreh* delivering the message
accompanied by soft tinkling bells
off-key trumpet blasts
clapping and stomping
whoops and whistles
the victorious
full orchestra

of *mechiyas Amalek*
by the Chosen ensemble.
At long last in grand conclusion and prose
singing the sweet rousing melody of Ancient
yet still so relevant today
Much like the *Shefoch Chamoscha*
said with great feeling on *Leil Haseder*,
Shoshanas Yaakov...
Stirring the soul for so much more
filling the heart with a yearning for unity once again.
kiymu vekiblu haYehudim*—may it be again soon!

SPRING

showers cleanse my soul...

Tax-Time Tale

Dedicated to my husband, Dovid, who is so much more than the BEST CPA!

Some
taxes make me weep
returns that slowly creep
papers clients keep
all for taxes
crunching numbers in my sleep
returns piled in a heap
fielding calls that aren't cheap
all for taxes

I feel like counting sheep
instead of counting...bleep
adding numbers in the deep
all for taxes

oh when will all this end
finding time for family and friend
making money just to spend
all for taxes

but then comes April 16th's day
I breathe and shout heartfelt "Hooray!"
this is a holiday
desk clean for all today
until next January...
Hey?!
All for the USA.
I am a proud CPA!!

Blue Angels

Waiting in line to get tested for what was a real eye-opener.

She stood there with her clipboard all dressed in blue
She stood there masked outside in the cold talking to you
She stood there with the line of cars for a while
In rain and sun, waiting patiently with a smile
She withstood doing something harder for her than for you
Saving lives is what you do when you're wearing blue
Oh, My Blue Angel!

He went to work masked up and in scrubs blue
He went to work Maimonides' mission to do
He went to work not just a nine-to-five job
He saved lives held hands felt the heart throb suppressing his sob
Oh, My Blue Angel!

Up in the sky where it's always blue
Are Angels fluttering around seeing all that you do
They count and they smile put your merits on the scale
They trumpet in Heaven all incoming good deeds "mail"
Of those blue angels without wings but still angels who fly
Whose prayers and actions they exemplify
Our doctors, our nurses, our Blue Angels, we salute
And thank you and bless you and pay most noble tribute

Dream On

Entering our seventh week of lockdown in the coronavirus pandemic, and our second week of Zoom/teleconference schooling, 3 Iyar 5781/April 26, 2020.

I dream of…
A world with no gloves
Masks cast aside
Smiles revealed
Eyes opened wide

I dream of…
No pretenses
I am who I am
You are who You are
Sing Dance Celebrate
In this kaleidoscope world
we are all shining stars

I dream of…
going back
and looking forward
to my classroom full of boys
In REAL time
Warm sticky energy
Life-filling noise

I dream of…
Visiting my mother
Going with her outside
Shabbos meals together
Filled with hard earned
nachas and pride

I dream of…
The mall!
Shopping so fun
Taking my girls out
Getting our nails done

I dream of…
No more illness
No more tears
No more worries
A new beginning
The end to our fears

I dream of…
babies
weddings
commencements
children finding their path Home
fluff-n-tulle 'n' monogram blessings
heart-swelling milestones

I dream of…
A world full of Light
Happiness healing so bright
Hands clasping *hands* together so tight
Embracing our Divineness with clarity and sight

I dream of…
Living the Dream

A Pesach Cleaning Sonnet

How do I get rid of chometz I wanna know!
Which cleanser is best in all those crevices to flow?
Take out the toothbrush the steelwool and *shmatte*,
gotta clean this house get rid of the clutter
For Pesach is coming and 'tis the season to expunge,
Not simple dirt, but leavened bread and contraband crumbs.
Vacuum, sweep or just plain old scrub.
Ay, my knees are achin' I sure need a back rub.
But I know there's more to this cleaning than just *shpritz* and wipe.
I know there's gotta be meaning somewhere in sight.
Beyond the boxes and bags of my coveted Pesach food,
I'm searching for something that generate an unleavened mood
No haughtiness or height in my bread that's for sure,
but maybe none of that belongs either in my attitude!
Humility, the soul ingredient in poor man's bread
may be exactly what I need to ingest and level my head.
Surely that crunch, most delicious sound on Pesach night,
is what the Greats had in mind for us to reach greater heights.
So gimmee that toothbrush steel wool and *shmatte*
gotta clean my soul get rid of the clutter
Vacuum sweep and do a good scrub
Tikkun hamiddos, ay, there's the rub.

The hills are alive and bleating.
Rolling mountains once green
Now cotton colored as far as the eye
        can see.
Dazzling brilliance in snow-white
        fluffiness,
Purity in animal form.

They come
gently pushing
softly mewing
and not so softly.
Treading lightly on tiptoes,
as if dancing,
yet with purpose in their stride.

Led by man
both eager to fulfill
their hallowed roles
in the Spring's Holiday and
Celebration of Freedom.

They flow into and with
throngs converging
at the market
filled with people bartering
buying and selling
for those in need.

Smells and sounds permeate the air
intermingling with
trumpets
spices
human voice
set against the backdrop of the constant
        "mehhh."

Closer and closer
they approach the ramp
the gates
the wide steps
the courtyard.
Flocking forward
like the very sheep they lead.

Pulsating with excitement
imbibing Holiness in every breath
as stillness settles upon all
with the vision of absolute white again,
Purity in human form.

Poised by the chamber
within the Heart of the Nation,
the Soul of the People,
Edifice of stone and gold,
where Heaven and Earth meet.
They have arrived.
And so has He.
*Ma navu al heharim raglei mevasser...**

* "How pleasant are the footsteps of the announcer on the mountains." (*Yeshayah* 52:7)

Why This Night

1. On this night...
At a table bequeathed in white
I sit like a queen newly coroneted
gazing out and beyond
the dancing flames
in candlesticks *en pointe*
gleaming silver reflecting
those most precious
revealing the luminescence
of my children's souls
glowing on their faces
on this Holiest of Nights

2. On this night...
with prayer so bright
for a world filled with Light
I proudly carry the flame of Continuity
like an Olympian torch bearer
passing it forward and onward
Proudly and Freely
to the next generation
fueled by the sparks of faith
lit so long ago and still burning now
On this Holiest of Nights

3. On this night...
Potential perfumes the air
scent of fresh flowers everywhere
princes and princesses cushioned on pillowed chairs
reclining, imbibing, poor man's bread grinding
reminiscing of family history legend and lore
darkened by slavery in days of yore
turning the tear-stained and purpled pages
we know what's in store
bitter and salty blend in with sweet
oh the joy of feeling so whole and complete
On this Holiest of Nights

4. On this night...
We dream of the Day
you and I come what may
stand all *together* each man 'neath his lintel his home
Awaiting the Prophet, we beckon and bellow
"*Shefoch chamoscha*!" and open the door
no matter how big or small that opening may be
it is our task alone who must venture forth sincerely
with help only from Heaven enlarging it as wide as can be
the time is late we've filled and drank the Four Cups of wine
the time is NOW and our fifth cup is still here biding its time
On this Holiest of Nights—*v'heiveisi*

Sometimes you want to jump in
but you can't
you don't like water
you're afraid to swim
you don't know how
so you think
instead you wait and watch the waves
oh how they roll and crash
you collect your courage
like the scattered seashells in the sand
miniscule shards intermingle with those
    still left intact
as you tiptoe along the edge
sea-spray your companion
toeing the shore
ever so daintily
stretching more boldly
a footprint embedded
proof of rebellion
now washed away
instantly
erasing exhibit A
of your bold attempt
was it really ever there?
and yet
it's time
to make that leap
You know it
you dare yourself
and how!
Run!
With all your might with all your soul!
Splash!
immersed completely
from head to toe

in cold wet
while reaching for a floor
that moves
where's the bottom
thrashing arms
what am I doing???
WHY?
oops
head submerges
guggling bubbles
eyes clenched tight
open pores tingle in salty fright
groping in the dark
grasping for a way out
climbing upward
air
aaahhh
breathing
swimming
graceful dancing
free-floating
ride the wave

Fire Works

Dedicated to the forty-five kedoshim, whose flaming souls returned to Hashem in Meron on Lag BaOmer 5781.

A flame is sent down below.
From Heaven it casts its fiery glow.
Yet no one can see this fire within,
the *neshamah* of the person,
the shining *pintele p'nim*.
But to feed it with good deeds it must!
The pure soul does truly trust
in its earthly vessel to fuel that flame
and light up for the world
Hashem's Holy Name.

Much like the *medurah*,
bonfire of Meron
that starts slowly and quietly
lighting
igniting
embers that BURN.

Timber upon timber
Stick upon stick
Adding faster and faster
As the flames quickly lick
Excitement building
as the sparks fly high.
Wild torches light up the sky.

Singing and dancing and reveling in the dark,
Oh to be part of that glow-in-the-Park!
The messages ablaze with each yellow-blue flicker.
Warming the crowds
joining in
heating up
swelling thicker
beating quicker.

The message of the torch once a spark
now a full beacon of fire,
oxygenates our Souls with Torah
propelling us higher and higher.
The message of the torch
a sputtering small spark
no matter how dim and dark.
An offering of fiery prayer is cast above
an offering consumed by fire and love.

The message of the torch
that it is but a spark no more
is to refuel and burst forth
from its Source
and soar.

May it be Your Will
never snuff its flame life still!
The message of the tiny flame
is that it
CAN
re-spark
re-ignite
BURN once again!

So much like that glorious *medurah* in Meron
where the fire stays lit and keeps going strong.
The final message as the fires die down,
glinting like precious jewels in a crown.
The passing of torch to torch reminds us of being kindled by one flame,
No matter how different we are really all the same.

Night is over and dawn begins,
we still dance
we still sing.
We rejoice with "*kol atzmosai*"* that Hashem is our King.
Yearning to be in our Holy Temple once more,
we pray to Him to expediently restore.

* "With all my might."

Holiness engulfed in a halo of the constant Fire,
accepting our prayers
our offerings
our spiritual desire

Forever we dance, forever we sing,
Together with Bar Yochai,
together with *Am Yisroel Chai*!

Sweatshirt skirt
Sneakers laced
plug myself in
to my sacred space
hit the dirt
pound the pavement
I escape to
my outdoor haven
thoughts are free
I am meant to be
Away from it allllll
Clear the air
Rain mixed with tear
Flowing down
Without sound
Release me
Ease me
Please me
Find the space within ME
And...
Dance in the Rain

Dual Curriculum

It's that time of year
and I always get that feeling
of mixed up
churned emotions,
unsettled mood.
Like a snow globe
that keeps shaking
with the snow whirling
twirling
swirling,
when will it stop?
And flutter gently to the ground
and stay.

I don't want it to end
and at the same time I do.
I am ready for a break
SUMMER VACATION!
But it's not even over yet and
Oh do I already miss those boys!
The noise
the chaos
the total fun
and awesomeness in newness.
Learning for the first time
under my watchful eye
in eagerness and anticipation,
and sometimes not.
Fraught with frustration.
CHALLENGING
situations
academic issues
BEHAVIOR.
Charts
Meetings
Always prayer.

And yet I love it.
The molding
the growing
the expansion of self
of myself
in knowledge
and of others and the world around him.

My dear precious student:
how I will miss you
and how grateful I am to have learned too,
from You!
Harbeh Torah lamadeti meirabbosai,
umeichaveirai yoser meihem,
umitalmidai yoser mikulam.*

* "I learned a lot of Torah from my teachers, and from my friends [even] more than them, and from my students more than all of them." (*Makkos* 10a)

SUMMER

umbrella of hope...

Desert Wander

Dry desert
Arid and hot
With miles of sand
Rippled like waves
As far as the eye can see
Sifting footprints
on golden granules
that peak and valley
and seem to touch
the ball of fire in the sky
that scorches
parched desperation
in search of
Water!
Mirage
a vision that dissipates
as quickly as it came
Despair
in this endless barren earth
and yet
Somewhere

a speck of green
a cactus!
Prickly
Barbed
Alone
It stands
It withstands
The searing constant heat
A wonder of nature
And G-d's glory
It's mystique
And beauty
Deep inside
Is water
Filling all its spines
That keep it straight
And nourished
Until...
It flowers
I am a Cactus

Flowers for your fancy
flowers of every kind
flowers that fill your senses
ease the difficulties of your mind.

Flowers that grow wild
flowers that grace your vase
delicate or exotic
they bring sunshine to your days.

Flowers that tickle you pink
flowers that are dramatic and make you think.
No matter what no matter where
flowers fill the air
with joy
delight
coloring life more bright.

Flowers that are holy whose presence fill the world
with purpose and beauty their testimony beholds
about a plain little mountain
that wasn't plain anymore.
A flower filled haven more than any floral store.
Budding, blossoming, transforming
fertile with lush green.
Aromatic
Dramatic foretelling something soon to be seen.
A mountain of splendor miraculously came to be
where the most climatic moment transpired
and time stood *still*
in our nation's history.

Flowers standing tall
and erect under the sun,
much like the Jewish People

stand together,
forever
as one.
Accepting and receiving with love and
humility
to do and live the will of G-d
for Mankind,
for Eternity.

Endurance

Upon reading a translated paragraph (for the first time!) from my father's manuscript of his experience with Mengele, I was inspired to write about my family.

To my noble Bobby and Zeidy, Fetters and Tantes, pillars in the sky.
To my endearing little cousins, fluttering angels on high:
Shavuos is coming.
And along with *zman matan Toraseinu* and savory blintzes,
it is time to think of you.
To take pause and reflect and remember our family's story.
A humble past, yet not so humble at all.
Simple and pure,
holy and sublime,
living in another time,
a lifetime ago.
That world now lost forever
yet eternally imprinted in my soul.
Your precious names and identities, like the bold black letters in a Torah Scroll
are etched in my heart
and sealed in the DNA we share.
Flowing through my blood and solidifying the marrow of my bones,
moistening my father's multicolored eyes that I too inherited
catalyzing salty tears to fall freely
and staining my cheeks wet with sadness and longing.
Drawing strength from survival of the Survivors
my tears intermingle with the sweet taste of the comfort of continuity
by bequeathing your precious names to grandchildren and great-grandchildren,
endowing them the precious legacy of their great forefathers and mothers,
ensuring the eternal permanence of your presence,
Your essence,
Your memory lives on.
*Yehei zeicher nishmos hakedoshim vahatehorim baruch.**

Inspired by my daughter's trip to Poland.

The images they haunt my mind
so peaceful looking now
forests
green grass
trees
neat buildings
winding paths
all witness to what was...
not peaceful
crisp starched cloth
shiny black boots
impeccable manners
oh so cultured
don't be fooled by the
blasphemous Nordic beast
with blonde hair and blue eyes
humanity at its worst
juxtaposed

Humanity at its most transcendent
martyrdom in purest form
for life
and dignity
and somewhere...
G-d
Miracles abound
kindness of others
from within
and without
tales too incredible to believe
but I believe
for I am one of those miracles.
And *so are you* my very precious dear
daughter.
your namesake lives on as does mine.

Yehudis Bas Chaim Meyer, *Hy"d*
Chana Bas Yitzchok Tvi, *Hy"d*
Maryam Bas Yitzchok Tvi, *Hy"d*
*Yehei zeicher nishmos hakedoshim vahatehorim baruch.**

* "May the memory of the souls of the holy and pure be blessed."

Tears of Toil and Till

This was written after reading about the Piacezner Rebbe, and after reading excerpts from the Holocaust diary of my father, who survived Auschwitz at the age of 15.

I cry for my People
I cry for our pain.
I cry for our Home,
will we ever see it again?

I cry for my family,
murdered not so long ago.
I cry for memories stolen,
precious stories I'll never know.

I cry for the bloodshed
of the old and the young.
of centuries of suffering,
heroes known, some unsung.

I cry for this seeming-endless *galus*
and of other exiles past.
I cry and wonder
how long will Concealment last?

I cry for our children,
those sick and those lost.
I cry for our tarnished purity
and pray at all cost.

I plead for my People
and try not to cry.
And yearn for the day when
I will smile with bright eyes.
Awakening from this slumber
like after a long bad dream.
I will cry *no more,*
only joyously sing!

*Shir hama'alos... hayinu kecholmim!**

**"A song of ascents...we will be like dreamers." (*Tehillim* 126:1)

Wandering
in this world
a sojourn of centuries
spanning the continents and seas
is our history

making our mark
and finding the Spark
within the shards
splintered since the dawn of time
we must restore creation's inner rhyme

so easy to get lost
and distracted
sidetracked and confused
where is the Path
laid down by our Fathers

the map lies unused
find the blueprint
and read the signs
that are here right before us
Torah guidelines

There all along
Shadowing us so strong
His Presence always here
whilst we are far from Him or near
inner compass won't let us shirk
our mission our task our life's work;
is
The Holy Wandering Jew

City of Dreams

I'm so tired,
yet it's moments like these that I yearn
and dream
vividly in Technicolor
and sometimes in sepia black and white

Take me to the place of my dreams
where the sun is so bright
and the breeze is so gentle
and the sweet sound of white doves
cooing
calling me
serenading me
with the flapping of their wings
flying on High
nestling in the greenery somewhere up there
and in between
cushioned by paper prayers

I am so close in my dreams
almost there
that I can practically feel the coolness
of those ancient stones
to touch them
and lean on them
dare to kiss them
how I wish to be there
but for now
and until Then,
You remain the City of My Dreams

Hineni

Inspired by a return trip to Eretz Yisroel after a fifteen-year hiatus.

Walking down those smooth worn steps
journeying UP in *Aliyah*
Fifteen years feeling like a lifetime
I am in total awe
Breathe and weep
behold the sweeping view
of our most precious
Sacred stones
Wall of strength
and legacy of Survival
      I am here!

Hugging my daughter
once twice
over and over
never stopping
Love encircling
Gratitude overflowing
for this moment
Zeh hayom asah Hashem*
birthday gift for eternity
      We are here!

Sitting on the stone slab
with a lunch of waffles and cream
food for the stomach and soul
holy and sweet
I delight
in the spiritual site
marveling at the Churvah
no longer a *churvah*
davening Minchah!
coming full circle
feelings so complete
      I am here!

Visiting family
the place where it all began
A Blessing from our Parents
I take my daughter's hand
May you be like Sarah and Rivkah
Rochel and Leah
And walk in their ways
burn your *own* candle so bright
remember these Heavenly days
From the flame lit long ago
by Avraham, Yitzchok, and Yaakov
Hold on tight never let go
      For we are always here

Take me to the place of Service of old
that stood before the Palace of Gold
Ancient Temple
Desert Travels
Judean Hills now its rest
listen closely
smell *ketores*
hear her whispered words
Chana's bequest
forged in our *mesorah*
Standing now forever as then
      I pray I am here

Across the globe we may all Rome
in exile
He too yearns
waits *with* us
oh so long...
for His children to return
Home
resting my head on that pillow rock

my tears my prayers flow without stop
feeling the gentle breeze in caress
birds cooing in the crevices
I implore and feel comforted in His Nest.
      I am finally here

People, People
from whence they come
why they come
seeking

seeing
believing!
pictures selfies they all stare
Feeling something in the air!
He is near:
      G-d is here!

*Ani ma'amin be'emunah sheleimah...v'af al pi
sheyismahmei'ah... ani ma'amin.***

---

* "This is the day Hashem made."

** "I believe with complete faith [in the coming of the messiah], and even though he may delay, nevertheless, I await him every day." (Prayer)

So long
seemingly endless
the Pain
of death
from illness
and loss
from destruction
of the psyche
torment of the soul
the wandering
directionless
Child
searching
for Something
other than
the chaos
of instability
and turmoil
Escape
the emptiness
fractured splinters

of something once Whole
you me we
Weep
Yearn
Seek

YET

from this tomb of exile
comes a whispering
listen closely
and smell the roses of
the sweet scent of
renewed hope
in G-d!
Revealing
Healing
Cleaving
Paving
for us the path
to come
Home.

Showers of Love

We think we know
we want it so
that life should be
what we dream so perfectly
always up and never down
convenient comfort without frown
and so it feels
static and surreal
when time has a way of moving slow
and suddenly so very fast
that now becomes then and a thing of the past.
What happened to all the happily ever after
with only the hollow echo of faded laughter
oh how we pine for perfect dreams
instead of tears and silent screams
Yet things can change in the blink of an eye
and just as quick with joyful cry
from whence it came
surprises reign
prodded by prayer
we are the lost wayfarer
Salvation comes like *restorative rain*
from our Father so dear
Always near
Always here
and now we know
Souls want it so
that Life is exactly how it should be
so Masterfully planned
for you and for me,
All Perfectly.

Bridge to Myself

Dedicated in the memory of
Avi Yaakov Mordechai ben Yitzchok Tzvi
Alte-zeide Yitzchok ben Yittel
Nagymama Daisy Bas Emma

Looking out the window
seeing the city's sights
through wizened eyes of life
remembering innocent child's delight
from atop the Margaret Bridge
linking past to present
filled with so many memories
a happy and sad goulash
in this land of Buda and Pest
much like the flowing river
an amalgam of pain and pleasure
Blue Danube once red
now a centrifuge of emotions
and flowing Memorial
to the Holy
HY"D

Bumping along
cobbled streets
gliding along
paved superhighways
paradox ride
cable cars
buses
trams
the underground
beware the closing doors!
people, people everywhere
seeing and not seeing
unsmiling they stare
haunted past

communist commiserations
still linger
distant revolution
freedom restitution
stale

Dutiful visits to
old buildings
divine architecture
city grime where's the grass
still we play hide and seek
in the park across the street
and who could forget
Fisherman's Peak?
climb the mountain
steps up to the castle Var
and back down to Nagymama
lazy days at Lake Balaton!

Fagyi sweet*
langos grease**
sugared *ribizli****
sour pitted cherries—ooh!
summer winter fall delicacies
I miss it so much
sometimes…

Flying from so far
a short visit
a lifetime
by plane and car
respects to pay

in Graveyards of old
black with gold
stone and marble
so cold
cry shudder and sigh
where have the years gone by?!?

Placing gently the worn rock
handpicked by progeny

so proud of our stock
time is stilled and stops
daven with all my might
please make everything all right
and in the eternal tranquility there
feel a closeness in the air
never give up hope do not despair
      "My daughter, I am always here."

*Hungarian slang for "ice-cream."

**A Hungarian dish—fried dough.

***Hungarian for "currants."

Like an aged bottle of wine
that gets better with time
or the excitement that comes anew
with the purchase of a pair of shoes
each one special a true treasure
whose value is beyond measure
that keeps us going
in times of joy and trials
a Source from which to draw strength and smiles
built upon a Foundation deep and strong
no matter if the years be few or long

The vintage ones are
flavored by years of togetherness
enriched by memories of shared past
bubbling with adventures and coming of age
inhaling the aroma of jubilant milestones
of throwing *that* white cap
oh so High
ready to fly
Israel
Life
here we come!

Walking down the aisle
baby's very first smile
with diploma in hand
on our own we proudly stand
our glass is filled, time distilled
First job
new neighbors
a big move
we shift we grow
adjust our youthful attitude
change in a whole organic way
meeting different people day to day

crossing the threshold of our lives
possibility an open door
we grow up and we
Pray

Navigating horizons and unchartered paths
situations that make us cry and laugh
and so we hammer and try to fix
this time with new "shoes" to kick
assembling buildings with brand new bricks
while cementing structures on fresh ground
taking in the novel view all around
creating establishing meaningful and sure
this precious edifice so secure
an abode that will endure
the tests of time
and my sappy rhyme—
is the beautiful House of Friendship

Kiss the *mezuzah*
I lovingly do
as I so gratefully appreciate
each and every one of You.
of course, with a brand-new pair of shoes!
L'chaim!

The Best One

Dedicated to the campers of Morah Camp!

I set out with my bag
trough-like around my neck,
anticipating the deliciousness of this
    outing.
On a beautiful summer day
the blue sky is dotted with my favorite
    clouds,
cumulus,
I eagerly embark on this quest to
accumulate.

There they are!
we shout with glee,
as we spy them
hiding in the green
waiting for Someone
to redeem them,
little bursts of red
and raven purple.

I salivate before I even taste,
savoring the experience of what's to
come—
isn't that half the fun?
Its most authentic form.

I reach for one
and see another,
darker,
plumper,
juicier.
Oh!

but it is so high,
Can I reach it?

I strain,
I stretch,
I do my best.
I aim High
and reach it.
This time.

I look some more
and search
through the brush of leaves
and tangle of branches.
I spy a whole cluster,
a family.
Sweet and delicious,
I grab the bunch
by the handful,
they are mine
but they are mine to share as well.
And I bestow them to my fellow picker
and friend.

Satisfied with our lot,
and happy with our friends' lot,
we all sit with contentment and
    contemplation
as we bask under the tree,
eating our cherries
and grasping on to the Tree of Life.

Firefly Delight

*With appreciation to **Binah** for publishing the original.*

I sit in stillness as the sun sets and the sky slowly darkens
Faint outlines of the clouds play hide and seek with dusk
Mothers calling to their children fade in the background
As accompanying pitter-patter of bare feet graze freshly mowed grass
Returning home
It's time for bed
Shower sprays and faucets spilling out clean
Washing away summer grime and that day's fun
Fresh PJs and softly combed hair
Tucked into a piece of downy heaven
With whispered prayers and love
Ode to sweet dreams
And for what tomorrow brings...
I breathe in honeysuckle and wait
For the Lite Brite of the nite
And the dancing in the dark
Dessert after coal and grill
Sweeter than a firecrackers pop(sicle)
Pitter-patter back out
Pajamas rumpled
My piece of heaven climbs into my arms
Trying to catch a flash of light
While I sit in stillness in the dark
With my whole heart
Oh, Summer...

Dream Cloud

My mind is adrift
like the clouds outside my window.
Warmed by the peeking sun
that is also settling itself into sleep,
I wish to leap out and join them,
enveloped and smothered by
their downy fluffiness and just drift...
Oh dear, I am rooted to the chair
self-imposed oasis of my bedroom
escaping the bedtime madness
for just a few moments if lucky
enjoying the peace and visage
of Cirrus, Stratus, Cumulus
figure skate in the sky
silently and serenely
I feel myself gliding
drifting away
on my own
Dream Cloud

Zzz...

Streaks of color
pink and orange
with a splash of yellow
rainbow sherbet Heaven
distracts my yoga stretch
as I look out in wonder
at the ever-changing
deepening intensity
breathtaking beauty
of the canvas that is the sky

Reflections of the moon
on gentle still waters
her white halo glistening
upon the blackest of ripples
outlining a dark floating…
         something—a duck!
echoing a chirp—a bird still awake!
soothing the end of day
and tucking in worries
far away from my mind

Scent of lilac
somewhere out there

tickles my nose alive
awakening it with inhalation
of that calming fragrance
breathing in deeply
filling my essence
with organic incense
feng shui of body and soul

Feeling with my whole being
Nature's four elements
Earth, Water, Fire, Wind =
Sand, aqua, embers, breeze
Squishing
Splashing
Tingling
my every pore and inner core
vitality oh so pure

Delighting
in life's simple pleasures
enhanced by ice-cold treats
and Hashem's beautiful World
Tasting refreshing and sweet
oh the joy of summer!

Kaleidoscope

Dedicated to the Chaburah.

Life is but a looking glass
reflecting light and refracting
exposing the vast color spectrum
of multihued facets that swirl
forming patterns and shapes
each distinct and unique
with endless variations
turning and twisting
in so many directions.
Of possibilities and choices
and Dreams that
confuse confound
astound
delight excite
Oh the frustration
in losing the original design!
One wrong revolution
and all is Dark
shuttering the Light
and the vast potential within
yet still right there within one's grasp
in the cracks that illuminate
hinting to the opalescent kernels
and seeds of optimism that lay in the shadows
is the ability and the gift
to hope for something bright
then stumble onto something else
more complex
more intricate
more beautiful
inspiring further probe
and search for more
Re-turn.

No twist of fate nor a play on words
but the rules of the game
and the reality
in this child's play
Double Entendre
and Game of Life
It's essence an object of enchantment
Re-shifting perspective once more
revealing the luminous Light
dazzling shades of translucency
kaleidoscope of brilliant Design
exposing what was always there,
the Master Plan
hidden and waiting
now in full transparency
finally joyously eternally
Discovered.

To speak to You
I used to think I had to cry
But now I know
All I need to do is *try*
To speak to You
I now know
Is a moment I won't forgo
Beginning with the rising sun
While those precious still sleep on
Those uttered words carry me through
Each morn till afternoon anew

Finally in the moonlight still
I whisper to You
Hopes and dreams to fulfill
As eyelids close and yawns asunder
Give thanks to You in my slumber
For the wonder
We call Life

My Gratitude knows no bounds.
Intertwined with nature of the heart,
it awakens the wintery slumber that is my life.
And defrosts the sterility of my stratosphere,
warming my numbness of mind and of feeling
back to existence,
spreading its welcoming warmth like a fuzzy blanket.
My Gratitude cleanses me like a fresh spring rain
showering my face in revitalizing tears—
tears once bitter wash cheeks
tasting refreshingly sweet.
Tears once restrained and locked up chained by vulnerability,
fragility,
fall freely from my eyes unleashing the ache in my soul,
watering my parched Spirit
as tiny buds of hope sprout into beautiful verdant green.
My Gratitude shines brightly like the summer sun
brilliantly, blindingly, radiantly.
Its rays reaching out far and beyond the oceans horizon
reflecting the deep blue waves of my ups and downs,
shimmering upon the tempestuous stormy waters of Challenge.
My Gratitude clings on in defiance
to the withering dried up leaves
despite the blowing winds of Fall.
No longer tenuous as it was in its sapling state,
its roots firmly grounded beneath the surface,
while pushing upward like the Redwood giant
now resplendent in all its glorious golden and rich colors.
And emerging like a victory flag after battle
waving forth its hues of strength and fortitude
in varying shades and tints of the human experience,
conditioned to the constant change that is
the Seasons of Life.

Glossary

Aliyah [to Israel] – moving to Israel

alte-zeide – great-grandfather

avi – my father

ba'al koreh – reader from the Torah scroll

bas mitzvah – a girl's coming of age, at twelve years old, when she becomes an adult according to the Torah and is considered responsible for her actions

Bobby – grandmother

chaburah – group

Churvah – historic synagogue in the Jewish Quarter of the Old City of Jerusalem that was destroyed in 1721 and rebuilt in 1837. It was destroyed again in 1948 by the Arab Legion, then rebuilt in 2010

Churvah – ruins of a building

davening – praying

Fetter – uncle

galus – exile

hamantasch – triangular shaped pastry, often filled with fruit, eaten around Purim

kedoshim – lit. holy ones; Jews who were killed by gentiles for being Jewish or for not agreeing to violate the Torah

ketores – incense offered on the alter in the Temple

Leil Haseder – Passover *seder*

Matan Torah – giving of the Torah on Mount Sinai

mechitzah – partition

mechiyas Amalek – eradication of Amalek

medurah – bonfire

Megillah – scroll containing the Purim story

mesorah – oral tradition

mezuzah – a small scroll affixed to the doorframe

Minchah – afternoon prayer

mitzvah – commandment

morah – teacher

nachas – pleasure

Nachshon [ben Aminadav] – name of the leader of the tribe of Judah when the Jews left Egypt; he was the first to jump into the Red Sea

nagymama – grandmother

nes – miracle

neshamah – soul

pintele p'nim – small spark of spirituality

Purim shpiel – Purim play

Shefoch chamoscha – opening words of a prayer said at the Passover *seder*, asking that G-d punish those who deny His existence

sheitel – wig

sheitel macher – wig styler

sheva brachos – seven blessings said over a cup of wine in honor of a new couple

shmatte – rag

Shoshanas Yaakov – prayer said after reading the Megillah on Purim, celebrating the salvation from Haman's decree

shpritz – spray

shul – synagogue

Tante – aunt

tikkun hamiddos – improving one's character

tuchter – daughter

vayechulu – the opening word in *Kiddush*, blessing the Sabbath over a cup of wine

Zeidy – grandfather

zman matan Toraseinu – the time that the Torah was given to us, i.e., Shavuos

About the Author

Judy lives in Baltimore, Maryland, with her husband and children. She likes to walk with the sunrise and watch the red cardinals in her backyard. In addition to writing, her passions are family and preschool children, where she has been working for two decades. Judy can be reached at seasonsoftherain@gmail.com.

CPSIA information can be obtained
at www.ICGtesting.com
Printed in the USA
BVHW02084709121
621074BV00006BA/432